PHOTOGRAPHIE

Louis CLERGEAU

PONT-LEVOY
LOIR-&-CHER.

PORTRAITS
REPRODUCTIONS
AGRANDISSEMENTS
SPÉCIALITÉ DE GROUPES

A Village in France

Translated from the French by Willard Wood
Editor, English-language edition: Lory Frankel

Library of Congress Catalog Card Number: 96–84380
ISBN 0–8109–3747–6

Printed and bound in France

A Village in France

Louis Clergeau's Photographic Portrait of Daily Life in Pontlevoy, 1902–1936

Text by Jean-Mary Couderc • Introduction by Nina Favard • Foreword by Paul Gottlieb

Harry N. Abrams, Inc., Publishers

Foreword

Let me introduce you to my home-away-from-home—a village in France called Pontlevoy—and tell you how I came there. I well remember the first time I saw the unpretentious country village located between the river Loire to the north and the river Cher to the south.

My friends Bert and Jeannie Salzman had decided to buy a house in France in 1977. After five years of living in Pontlevoy for part of every year, they settled there full-time in 1982. For years they kept inviting me to visit. I had been drawn back to France time and again since my first magical journey in 1956, when I worked in a Paris travel agency by day and patrolled the bars and jazz clubs near the boulevard Saint-Germain by night. It was not until 1984 that I found myself on a business trip to Paris in late winter with a spare day to see Bert and Jeannie.

A comfortable express train going southwest from the Gare d'Austerlitz took about ninety minutes to bring me to Blois. I stepped down to the platform and saw Bert—looking like the quintessential French farmer. Faded blue smock, dark blue cap, grizzled beard, and twinkling eyes (no wonder that some time later Bert was cast as Monsieur Fromage in a French cheese television commercial, despite the fact that he had at best a shaky command of his adopted language. To get to Pontlevoy we drove through the handsome provincial town of Blois, past the approach to its great château and down the main street lined with shops and set off by neat flower beds. The street took us to a stone bridge arching across the Loire. As we turned right and followed the road along the southern bank of the river, the skyline of the town—cathedral dome, château, and houses—was perfectly lit by the sun, as if for our pleasure.

Bert and Jeannie lived in a cozy five-hundred-year-old farmhouse surround-ed by fragrant rosebushes in summer. When I arrived, the garden beds offered leeks. From inside, sitting at the table looking out through the Salzman's front door, I could see the spire of a thousand-year-old abbey, the slate roofs of houses and shops, and, above, a vast, blue-gray sky. There was something peaceful and compelling about this view—something that was having an almost physical effect on me.

After a lunch of perfectly roasted chicken in Bert and Jeannie's combination living room, dining room, and kitchen, warmed by a fire burning in the small hearth, Bert and I went to see the notary, who, among other functions, handles real estate transactions in provincial France. I had not been looking for a house anywhere, but for some months, as the age of fifty approached, I had been thinking that it made sense to consider where I might retire one day. Whether it was the view out the Salzman's front door or Jeannie's roast chicken, a *coup de foudre* struck in Pontlevoy. I suddenly knew I wanted to buy a house in this place. As I recall, Maître Berger had more than one prospect to offer but he strongly suggested I look at the Fabre house. "The old man has been dead for two years and his children don't seem to want it," he said. We walked through the narrow, winding main street, down the hill past the abbey and the village church, to an open place called the *champ de foire*, the fairgrounds or marketplace. At one corner stood a small plinth bearing the bust of the discoverer of a new breed of sheep.

Pontlevoy is at the center of a gently rolling agricultural terrain, whose residents annually celebrate the *Fête du Mouton* (sheep festival). The *Champ de Foire*, charming in name, is now a large macadam parking lot for people visiting the village, perhaps to see the museum of heavy vehicles, or for locals coming to church on Sunday. Every weekday it also accommodates huge trucks during lunch hours because facing the square, and adjoining what would turn out to be the house I would buy, sits the Hermitage, a *routier*—what we call a truck-stop restaurant. Not the most elegant cuisine is served, but for a modest price, a hearty lunch of appetizer, entrée, fruit, cheese, dessert, and red wine is offered to an appreciative assemblage of truck drivers and certain local artisans and bargain hunters who gravitate particularly toward the small bar. Bert and I walked past the restaurant, and there, flanked by two stone pillars, stretched a rusting fence with a gate to a driveway beyond. A rusted bellpull didn't work.

An old iron key unlocked the gate and we walked around the overgrown circular driveway into a property that enchanted me at once. Entering the stone house through the front door and passing quickly through the central hall I opened the door that gave onto the back garden—and I was instantly captivated. I had always loved the garden of Tolstoy's town house in Moscow—much larger than what I saw now, but similar: a rectangular property with grand old trees growing within a central grassy oval edged by a gravel path that wound among lilac bushes, laurels, cherry trees, and an exotic bamboo thicket. At the very back of the property a small stream, or *vivier*, now stocked with fat goldfish, ran from one side to the other. The weather was cold and it was many months before I learned there were also rosebushes and grapevines and espaliered fruit trees growing against the walls that bordered the property. Yet even in the cold of early spring I felt the pull of these tranquil acres.

Sometime later one of the first visitors I welcomed there was Eleanor Perenyi, a gifted writer on gardens and nature, who came with her friend Mary McCarthy and Mary's husband, Jim West. I knew them only casually, but hearing that they were traveling south from Paris, had invited them to lunch. I think they stopped out of curiosity. Before lunch, Eleanor walked around the garden, looked at me, and said, "I hate you; you don't know what you have." She was struck by the amazing variety of old fruit trees, species she thought no longer existed: apples and pears that were trained to grow in every style of espaliering fruit trees. But I had known right away how special a place I had found in Pontlevoy.

Realizing that I would never use the house more than six months a year, in the days following my discovery of the house I decided to find a partner to buy a half interest. I spoke to French cousins in Paris and to two families in New York. Hugh Nissenson, my college roommate and friend, and his wife, Marilyn, were immediately intrigued by the idea. By chance, they were planning a visit to France two months after my first visit to Pontlevoy. They saw the house and agreed at once to join in.

From the moment we took up residence, our experience proved false the cliché about the unfriendliness of the French. Perhaps because Bert and Jeannie had established themselves so happily, by the time we arrived we were simply accepted as friends of the Salzmans and made to feel welcome. There were neighbors who helped us find contractors to renovate and repair the house, and there was Monsieur Ducros the *kinésithérapeute* who saved me from a painful back attack. In time we met a town full of warm and hospitable people of whom the mayor, Monsieur Favard, and his wife, Nina, were outstanding examples. Both were professors of science in Paris, and M. Favard also served as a dedicated and committed mayor of our village. The Favards lived at the end of our street in a delightful and fertile property (which produced, among other crops, the best-tasting, fattest raspberries I have ever eaten). It had once been the village police station. Favard loved Pontlevoy and was particularly helpful to the several American families that had stumbled upon this out-of-the-way haven. It was M. Favard who found the photographs that make this book such a unique record of times gone by. Strolling the streets of Pontlevoy one day, he noticed, outside the home of the Clergeau family, boxes set out for collection by a club to which the contents were being donated. The boxes were filled with thousands of the original glass plate negatives in which old M. Clergeau and his daughter had captured image after image recording the life of the village, from the beginning of the century. Favard realized what a treasure these boxes contained and persuaded Clergeau's son to let the museum of Pontlevoy take custody of this rare photographic record of a village in France.

When I first saw the photographs, I understood more clearly my attraction to this place, which seems so little changed since M. Clergeau's early images made nearly a century ago: the same modest proportions of scale, the same dignified faces of the people. Although M. Favard did not live to see the publication of this book, Nina Favard worked long and hard to organize the material and I have had the pleasure of introducing her and the project to the French publisher Hervé de La Martinière. I hope you enjoy this superb selection of the Clergeau photographs, and I bid you welcome to "my" village. Welcome to Pontlevoy!

February 1996
Paul Gottlieb

Contents

Introduction

A Village and Its Photographer

When Louis Clergeau, a watch-maker-jeweler, moved to Pontlevoy in 1902 and opened a store there, no one imagined the consequences this would have. In this prosperous village, a number of businesses operated within the hamlet. The arrival of a new artisan was nothing to impress this hardworking rural population, busily going about its customary round of activities. And yet it is thanks to Louis Clergeau, then twenty-five years old and newly married, that the life of the village during the years that followed would be recorded in pictures and passed on to posterity.

In fact, the new arrival was not the average watchmaker-jeweler. Since adolescence he had harbored a passion for photography. He therefore supplemented his work repairing watches, in which he took a moderate interest, with professional photography, a practice he engaged in happily and with enthusiasm.

It was to be the start of a long journey. At the time he set himself up in business, few people owned a camera. People who wanted to preserve images of themselves or their families, whether in the context of daily life or an important family event, called in a professional. Celebrations—and there were many of them—were often documented as well, and the photographs made into postcards.

In subsequent years, photography became more generally practiced. The demands of clients evolved while the photographer's personality developed, all of which can be traced in his work.

Louis Clergeau had two children: a daughter, Marcelle, born in 1903, and a son, Jacques, born in 1910. Marcelle showed a deep interest in photography from adolescence, having been introduced to it by her father. Under his influence from the outset, when she became his partner in 1921, she scrupulously adopted his methods of work.

After Clergeau died in 1964, Marcelle preserved the collection of glass plates in her home—although, unfortunately, she kept them in an attic that proved not totally watertight. When she in turn passed away in 1984, my husband, Pierre Favard, who was then the mayor of Pontlevoy, and myself, both fascinated by this archive and long convinced of its importance, worked closely with Jacques Clergeau, Marcelle's brother, to preserve it. When we discovered the true greatness of the photographs, thanks to prints produced on the spot with a bor-

Before he moved to Pontlevoy, Louis Clergeau was photographed with his bicycle, to which his first camera, a Photo Hall, is strapped.

Louis Clergeau's Youth

rowed enlarger, we experienced a moment of great emotion and happiness. Each of the photographs more than fulfilled the promise held out by the numerous postcards by Louis Clergeau we had been collecting and the information we had gathered from Marcelle Clergeau, whom we had the privilege of knowing at the end of her life. She had spoken nostalgically and with great vividness (she was an excellent storyteller) about the happy years of her youth when she worked with her father, for whom she always had a profound admiration and felt much tenderness. "If only someone might become interested in Pontlevoy's past..." she was in the habit of saying. We did not know at the time that, long afterwards, we would take part in realizing her dream, which rapidly became our own.

Louis Clergeau was born in Pontlevoy on August 25, 1877. His father, Auguste, also a native of Pontlevoy, was gardener at the Collège de Pontlevoy, a very well-regarded Catholic secondary boarding school housed in the abbey. Shortly after his son's birth, Auguste changed jobs and became gardener at the Château de Saint Aignan. It was there that his son grew up, went to school, and underwent his apprenticeship as watchmaker-jeweler, the trade his parents had determined for him.

His schooling complete, Clergeau went to work for a watchmaker in Ecueillé, a village close to Saint Aignan, then for another in Coulommiers.

He probably became interested in photography at a very early age, since he bought his first camera in 1894, when he

Louis Clergeau's store in 1906. His photographs are on display at right.

9

Louis Clergeau often published postcards using his photographs. These, dated in the 1930s, show the rue de Chaumont and the Grande Rue and carry the credit "Image Clergeau, Pont-Levoy." Pontlevoy's name would be written without a hyphen from the end of World War II.

was seventeen. It was a 9 x 12 Photo Hall, which he would strap firmly to his bicycle in order to crisscross the countryside in search of landscapes to photograph.

He also took pictures of his friends and family. It is easy to imagine that on an employee's salary Clergeau had trouble financing what was a very expensive pas-

time, given the great cost of glass negatives. A few of his amateur photographs, taken between 1895 and 1900, have survived. Already his talent is apparent.

Pontlevoy and the Prewar Years

After he opened his shop in Pontlevoy, Clergeau was obliged to pursue his photographic activities professionally, so he needed to demonstrate his abilities in that field. He equipped himself first with a 13 x 18 camera, then with an 18 x 24, and installed a darkroom in his cellar. As electric lighting did not come to Pontlevoy until 1913, Clergeau lit the darkroom using kerosene lanterns fitted with red filters.

The photographer maintained a minutely detailed inventory of his photographs (though not all of them are included in it). He numbered them in chronological order and recorded them in small classroom notebooks. These documents offer highly valuable information, as they help us follow the evolution of the photographer's work, which was closely linked to the evolution of the village and the society in which he practiced his art.

The most affecting work dates from 1902 to 1914. It was during this time that Louis Clergeau was fine-tuning his work methods and his talent found its best expression. And the circumstances were most favorable then; the general craze for photography had reached the countryside and clients were beginning to request photographs not just of weddings and first communions but for a wider variety of circumstances and in greater number. Despite the particularly hard living and working conditions, the spirit of the times was carefree, and people liked to celebrate and have a good time. When aviation came to Pontlevoy in 1910, the enthusiasm rose to such a pitch that Clergeau's photographic records of local events were finally published as postcards. The photographer

PONT-LEVOY. - La Rue de Chaumont

Cliché Clergeau, Pont-Levoy

PONT-LEVOY. - La Grande Rue

Cliché Clergeau, Pont-Levoy

was young and dynamic. Not long after his arrival, he decided to free himself further by hiring the first of the four journeyman watchmakers who would help him in the shop over the years. Such were the circumstances in which a pictorial chronicle of life in the village of Pontlevoy came to be created.

During this time, Clergeau seems to have been most inspired when he was photographing his subjects in open spaces—in fields, in the countryside, or in the streets. His innate sense of composition led him to conceive full-blown tableaux in the manner of a painter. He placed the figures harmoniously (even the dogs that always seem to be on hand!) as well as the farm equipment and tools, integrating them into a landscape whose broad lines he had carefully chosen. His photograph of a fishing party, for instance, is a minor masterpiece that calls to mind Jean Renoir's film *A Day in the Country*. His threshing scenes and harvest scenes demonstrate a remarkable equilibrium between the figures and their environment, the aesthetic effect always taking precedence over strict verisimilitude in the matching of people and objects for the purposes of the photograph. Those in the group photographs

were clearly anxious to show themselves to best advantage to the camera, which they considered a slightly mysterious object, and seem conscious of the ceremony's importance: "We're having our picture taken!"

At this time, the photographer's talent was finding expression in a wide variety of themes: bird's-eye views of streets in which passersby are stopped for an instant, the arrival of the little train at the Pontlevoy station, packed with passengers, met by a large crowd for the aviation festival of 1910. In the foreground, the straw boaters and flower-bedecked hats of the enthusiastic spectators clearly signal the magnitude of the event.

Clergeau's strengths also found happy expression in images of artisans practicing their trade. Since interiors could not yet be lit sufficiently by artificial light, everything had to be photographed outdoors. A workshop, for instance, would be recreated outside for the occasion, and the photographer could then arrange with humor and tenderness some of the characters he knew so well. This resulted in superb photographs, such as Firmin Meunier and his portable winepress, which also included Auguste Clergeau, by trade a seedsman, at right.

Pages from an inventory book belonging to Louis Clergeau in which he entered the date and subject of each of his images, as well as their number in order. These books were kept continuously except for the years between 1914 and 1918—that is, during World War I, when the photographer was called up for active service.

Portrait of a family from Monthou-sur-Bièvre in 1911.

Louis Clergeau and his family, photographed while he was on leave in 1917. He wears the blue uniform and cap of the infantry. Young Jacques wears a sailor outfit, a popular mode of dress for children at the time.

The profession had its dictates, however, and Clergeau could not always give free rein to his aspirations. In taking group photographs, which became his specialty, he had to work within the constraints of the genre, namely to present as harmoniously as possible a number of people within a restricted space.

When setting up these photographs, Clergeau would devise a structure that reflected perfect symmetry within the group, a symmetry that was sometimes conventional. In a wedding photograph, for instance, for which he generally used 18 x 24 plates, the entire cast of characters had to be positioned according to protocol: the newlyweds themselves, the maids of honor, close family, distant family, and finally friends, not forgetting that age also had to be taken into consideration. In photographs of family groups, which usually presented three generations, the patriarch was generally seated in the center of the picture, his descendants standing around him in token of their respect, an arrangement that also provided Clergeau the symmetry he found so important. In his slightly stiff wedding pictures, Clergeau always managed to insert a touch of humor: a fiddler and his instrument in the foreground; a small figure looking down on the assembly from a dormer window; a mischievous guest holding a bottle and lifting his glass to the wedding couple.

The Pontlevoy photographer excelled at making group photographs, and he was often called on to perform this task. Even neighboring villages drew on him for his services, and he traveled around the countryside on his trusty bicycle. In photographing less formal groups, Clergeau still employed symmetry, but he also sometimes allowed fantasy to take over. His pictures of the Francs-Buveurs, or drinking club, and those of the yearly band of conscripts are joyful; the group shot representing the Proletarian Social Economy from the village of Thenay is perfectly relaxed.

The war, which erupted in 1914, brought this fine momentum to a halt. Clergeau was mobilized and his professional activities ceased until 1919. Since his arrival in Pontlevoy, he had taken 1,300 photographs, but only two survive from the war years, both showing him on leave with his family, wearing a Zouave's uniform in 1915 and a poilu's in 1917.

The Postwar Years and the Entry of Marcelle Clergeau

When Louis Clergeau returned to his career in 1919 he was forty-two years old. Little by little, he rediscovered his happy gift for photography by applying the same methods as before, but many changes had taken place, both in people's outlook and in the life of the village.

The little inventory notebook, in which he started keeping records again as soon as he resumed photographing, shows that no festive events were held in Pontlevoy in 1919 or 1920. The village emerged from the war, as did all of France, deeply wounded by the terrible struggle and mourning for its dead. A few weddings were celebrated; a particularly moving one shows the bridegroom, a poilu, wearing his military uniform for the occasion. During those two years, Clergeau photographed mainly family events. We learn from the little notebook that identification photographs came into existence at that time. Unknown in Pontlevoy before 1914, with the new crop of war widows and invalids receiving pensions, they had become a necessity.

Identification photographs were made by lining up several people in the same exposure and trimming the picture into individual images once the print was made. The veiled expressions of these mourning men and women give a discreet indication of their suffering, which was common to the country as a whole.

It was in 1919, however, that Clergeau photographed the American military band, with its superb musical instruments, in Pontlevoy, also evoking, though on a joyous note, the end of the war.

Starting in 1921, life began to return to a more normal level, and Clergeau's activities reflect this. His records show that he took more than twice the number of photographs that year than in 1920. Family ceremonies grew more numerous, and there were more festive occasions to document as well. That year, images were made of agricultural activities, parades, gymnastics groups, and school events; the photographer once again had the chance to express the many facets of his talent. The image of children putting on a play outdoors on the grounds of the girls' primary

Portraits taken by Louis Clergeau. On the back of each is an illustrated announcement designed by his wife, as well as the inventory number of the negative.

school, for instance, is remarkable for its composition.

In 1922, Louis Clergeau made a documentary record of the public primary school in Pontlevoy. It called for using a technique he was particularly fond of, which was to reconstruct outdoors activities that would normally take place inside the school. A medical checkup, for example, was set up in the playground. The picture humorously presents the doctors examining their young patients with stethoscopes and other instruments; at the same time, it testifies to the interest in preventive medicine.

It was during this same period that Louis Clergeau turned to his daughter, Marcelle, then eighteen years old, for help in dealing with his increased work load. He taught her the techniques of photography, and for several years she participated discreetly in his work, helping him to fill the growing demand for identity photographs and assisting in the process of taking family photographs.

She would also accompany her father whenever he went off to document an event or activity and learned from him how to perform this type of work. Only in 1926 did she become a full partner. In 1929 she attended training workshops, learning, in particular, how to retouch prints. Young, enthusiastic, and bold, Marcelle was on the lookout for new ideas. It was she who recreated the village's main street in pictures, taking a photograph of each store facade with the shop owners and their employees.

Louis Clergeau's career as a photographer suffered a reversal in 1933. Deeply affected by the death of his wife, he took few photographs that year, and his activities remained at a low level until his retirement in 1936. The last line written in his own handwriting in the little inventory notebook refers to an identity photograph. It is assigned the number 4,779.

Marcelle Clergeau Extends Her Father's Work

Marcelle now took on all by herself the role of village photographer. Her brother, Jacques, assumed the running of the store, still operated as a watchmaker-jeweler's. Sometimes Jacques helped Marcelle in making identity photographs. She remained very active until 1939, invariably called on to photograph family ceremonies, in Pontlevoy and the surrounding area, and she also documented special events, such as the 1938 cavalcade in Pontlevoy. However, the number of such festivities was declining, as French society was changing and new distractions evolved every day.

After World War II broke out in 1939, few photographs other than routine ones were made again until 1944, or even later; there was an exploding demand for identity photographs, whose interest today is largely documentary. An exception was the arrival of the American forces in Pontlevoy in October 1944.

In this photograph of 1922 in front of the Café du Commerce, Marcelle Clergeau appears in the center, to the right of her friend Rolande Berlu. The café, at the time run by Rolande's mother, is still in existence.

Marcelle made three fine photographs of the event, showing the troops' arrival, the saluting of the flag, and the ceremony at the monument to the dead.

During the 1950s, Marcelle saw her activities as a photographer once again grow more diverse. The photographs from this period show the profound changes that had occurred in French society since her entry into the profession, changes that succeeded each other at an accelerated pace in the years after the war. In their faces and general aspect, people appear more relaxed. Living conditions were not as hard, and everyone enjoyed a certain level of comfort. Social constraints were eased and life was lived with a new and growing freedom. On another level, photography was becoming commonplace, and the arrival of a professional photographer no longer produced the excitement it once had. Marcelle gradually worked less and less. She stepped down from the role of village photographer for good in 1963, having reached the age of sixty.

In all, Louis and Marcelle Clergeau produced more than ten thousand photographs of Pontlevoy and the neighboring region. Most were taken during the first half of this century, a period rich in historical events and marked by two world wars, during which technology and collective lifestyles evolved with unprecedented rapidity.

What is profoundly original in the work is its unity. For one village to have been observed and translated into pictures by a single photographer over such a long period is to my knowledge unique in the photographic tradition.

The photographs taken by Louis and Marcelle Clergeau unquestionably have great value for the documentary evidence they offer. But the work is particularly touching for its aesthetic value, its simplicity, and its authenticity. As it shows us men and women from the past, it also shows us ourselves and finds an echo in our secret garden. This explains why it so moves us.

Nina Favard

The Café Restaurant de la Poste in 1955 during "Pontlevoy's Big Week" in 1955. This establishment is still in existence.

A photograph taken in 1932 in front of Clergeau's store and the Café du Commerce, on the place du Collège, shows officials leading the Veterans' Day celebration. The poster advertises synthetic fertilizers from the Saint-Gobain factories.

A Village in the Heart of France

At the Center of a Great Plain

Early Aviation
and the Pontlevoy Airfield

The Great War
and the American Presence

The area of Pontlevoy fills a fan-shaped clearing bounded on the west and south by the Sudais and Montrichard woods. The town sits on a flat plain, some 330 to 400 feet (100 to 120 meters) in altitude, overlying extremely hard Beauce limestone, which was still supplying Pontlevoy with its handsome building stone at the beginning of this century.

The land register preserves a reference to the "Field of Battle" in memory of an engagement fought on July 6, 1016, in which six thousand men belonging to the comte de Blois and the lord of Pontlevoy were killed.

Known by the locals as "the plateau" or "Pontlevoy's little Beauce," this plain with its heavy soils came under cultivation only toward the end of the nineteenth century after first organic and later chemical fertilizers became available. As in Beauce, some farms still kept great flocks of sheep at the beginning of this century as a way of using stubble fields and fallow lands productively. Only gradually did the golden harvests that brought wealth to its farmers cover the plain.

At the time, a vineyard stretched from the slopes of the Cher to the countryside of Contres. This is a region in which the gamay grape grows well, as does sauvignon and two grapes known locally as *le côt rouge* and *le gros noir*, the latter, also called "the dyer," used to produce blended wines, especially near Saint-Romain. The small vineyard sheds that one still finds in the vicinity of Thenay or Montrichard bear witness to the former size of the vine-growing region, whose grape-picking harvests contributed another occasion for conviviality.

Images of the Village

The traveler approaching Pontlevoy from Montrichard first sees two church towers, one belonging to the parish church, the other to the "chapel," as the church of the abbey is known. These mark the site of the abbey, with most of the houses in the village clustered to the west of it. Built of gray stone, the houses are somewhat severe in appearance. The more prosperous habitations present a mellower face, being built of stone from Bourré, the same material that, with the help of the sun, gives an ocher glow to the handsome facade of the abbey. North of the parish church of Saint-Pierre, with its Roman tower and apse, is old Pontlevoy, with a commercial district as well as town houses from the fifteenth, sixteenth, and seventeenth centuries, the jewel being the early-seventeenth-century Dauphin's house, with its resplendent sun carved in the center of the facade. Most of the other houses date from the nineteenth century and speak of a prosperous era in the village's history that was largely due to its Catholic boarding school; schoolboys had so little time off that the families of the wealthier among them built town houses in Pontlevoy so as to spend as much vacation time as possible with their children.

The abbey, founded in 1034, was a large Benedictine monastery, enlarged in 1688 for the benefit of the school, which had opened in 1644. From its inception, however, the abbey offered instruction. The buildings that we admire today, 260 feet in length and dominating the terrace and gardens, date from the eighteenth century, the main one from 1701 to 1704 and the one angling westward toward the village (partially screened by a cedar planted on the day of Louis XVI's coronation) from 1755. In the latter building, the visitor will find the local museum, dedicated to three themes relating to Pontlevoy's past: advertising for the chocolate industry (Auguste Poulain, the famous chocolate maker, was born in Pontlevoy in 1825); early aviation (Pontlevoy had one of Europe's first airfields, built in 1910); and the Clergeau photograph collection. The abbey church, burnt down in 1263, was rebuilt in the fourteenth century only to have part of the nave destroyed during the Hundred Years' War, hence the present "chapel" corresponding to the original choir.

Louis Clergeau's postcards give an accurate picture of the village streets and squares, as little has changed in the meantime. Forming an arc between the Place de la Libération and the place de la Poste, the rue des Singes traces the outline of an ancient fortification. The old village center where the castle once stood is now crossed by the main shopping street, the Grande-Rue, renamed the rue du Colonel Filloux. Modern arteries form a square around the narrow heart of the village and the abbey, while the streets beyond are laid out at right angles and have more recent homes with small gardens or residential lots.

A Short-lived Station

A steam-driven tramway was inaugurated on October 25, 1900, to provide service between Montrichard and Blois, with a stop in Pontlevoy. The narrow-gauge railway under the regional authority of the Loir-et-Cher department was operated by the company T.L.C. (Tramways de Loir-et-Cher) and later, when electricity replaced steam, by T.E.L.C. Whenever possible, the tramway ran alongside the road. From Monthou-sur-Bièvre it followed the Blois road to Pontlevoy and from there the road to Montrichard, even on the winding section through the forest. The old "serpentine" or "crate," as it was called, made two round-trips a day. It was replaced in 1930 by an electric railway car, but the line was shut down shortly afterward, on July 1, 1934. The electric tram allowed a generation of Pontlevoy's inhabitants to go to the movies on Sundays in the canton's chief town. On the way back, going up the hill from Montrichard, the young would hop out and run beside the car. The tramway seems to have had a strong impact on the local economy and to have opened Pontlevoy to both the administrative center of the canton and the main town of the department. The gap left by the loss of the tram line was left unfilled until after the war, when automotive transport came into widespread use.

Early Aviation and the Pontlevoy Airfield

An airfield was built in Pontlevoy in 1910. It operated until the war broke out in 1914 and sporadically afterward until 1918. In spite of its brief existence, it meant a great deal to the region. From 1913 it was listed in the Yearbook of International Aeronautics as one of about forty airfields in Western Europe.

In June or July of 1910, a pilot and mechanic from Paris, Fernand Morlat, talked a rich local farmer, Charles Tauvin, into building an airfield. They chose a site less than a mile from the center of the village on a relatively narrow forty-five-acre strip of land. Morlat arranged for the same landowner to provide him with a former sugar beet factory to use as a shop for the construction of airplanes and automobiles. Louis Clergeau photographed a prototype in 1910 that was probably built by Morlat. A capable instructor, Morlat gave flying lessons to students who came down from Paris and even from abroad, and he demonstrated an instinct for business and public relations. The inhabitants of Pontlevoy came to the airfield to see him fly, and the press regularly published reports on his flight times: ten minutes, then twenty . . .

Gradually winning over Charles Tauvin (and his family) to the cause of aviation, Morlat persuaded him to pay for the hangars, airplanes, and "school of aviation." The two men then quarreled bitterly, and in February 1912, Tauvin sold the lot to a certain Roberthie, a propeller manufacturer from Saint-Cyr-sur-Loire. The transaction, notarized by Maître Ledoux of Pontlevoy, included "the school of aviation, consisting of its name and clients, rights to the leasing agreement, the deals under development, the students presently enrolled," as well as various aircraft, such as "a Blériot monoplane with an Anzani motor, a Nieuport monoplane with a Darracq motor, a Voisin biplane with an E.N.V. motor, a taxi with an Anzani motor made for learning the rudiments, the wings being too short to take off, an orange Poulain biplane, dismantled, with a

Laborp motor, a Blériot fuselage."

All of which shows that the airfield had become remarkably well-equipped in a very short time. One surprising clause stipulates that the new owner was not to hire F. Morlat or to let him onto the airfield, even as a spectator to a free air show. A deed for the lease of the field and hangars bears the same date. There were at first two hangars parallel to the road, then three more built on an angle as military aircraft began to make frequent stopovers at the field.

French military aviation came into being in September 1909, after the great international air show at Reims. Lieutenant-colonel Estienne, later to become the father of the military tank, initiated a certificate for pilots at Vincennes in August 1909. Some twenty men passed the test in 1910, ten of them officers from the Farman school in Châlons. Military aircraft appeared in Pontlevoy as early as 1912, particularly during the Western Maneuvers. The airfield was still in use during the war. G. Chenneveau recalls hearing an aircraft circle overhead one day, and, realizing that the pilot was trying to land, he took two five-liter cans of gas out to the airfield for him. He still remembers seeing the pilot's mustache caked with ice. The American forces used the field for a time before establishing their base

in Romorantin-Pruniers—in fact, an American landed on a barn in the village, destroying a whole corner of it, and was taken away swathed in bandages in a sidecar.

Fernand Morlat had a talent for public relations and the celebration he organized on August 14 and 15, 1910, to inaugurate the new airfield is still remembered. A leafy arch of triumph was erected over the road from Blois and sumptuously decorated. On Sunday, August 14, the brass band filed by on parade, and when bad weather made flying impossible, Morlat taxied his plane up and down the airstrip. The *Républicain du Loir-et-Cher*, whose editor-in-chief was the regional writer Hubert-Fillay, published an account on August 18 of the reception that greeted the departmental prefect at the station, mentioning the many trains laid on for the occasion. In 1911, two of the pilots in the Paris-Madrid airplane race landed at Pontlevoy: Divetain, whose Goupy aircraft turned over on takeoff, and Gibert, in a Blériot. Gibert was forced to wait for a long time on the ground after a fatal accident to the minister of war, Berteaux, and an injury to the president of the state council when the pilot Train missed his takeoff at Issy-les-Moulineaux, which almost led to the cancellation of the race.

The airfield's fate was officially sealed by the end of 1912. A letter dated November 22 from the office of the minister of war, written in response to a query from the district deputy Joseph-Paul Boncour, states that the airfield was in all respects suitable for landings but that the army did not have the funds to maintain the hangars, though it hoped the township and department would do so.

What survives of this saga is contained in the remarkable photographs of Louis Clergeau and in the museum exhibit, whose model of the airfield was built from plans reconstructed by the engineer J. Pécard, to whom we owe a great deal of information.

The Great War and the American Presence

With a few rare exceptions, the war that ravaged Europe from 1914 to 1918 left no direct traces in the work of Louis Clergeau. The photographer himself went off to war and only resumed his activities in January 1919. Indirect traces, however, include wedding photographs showing grooms with emaciated faces wearing soldiers' uniforms, perhaps released from the hospital in 1919 or 1920; photographs of incomplete family groups, the women in mourning or half mourning; and the moving image of a child from Sambin preparing to take first communion in 1922 who wears the decorations of a father who died in the war (a highly unusual practice in Touraine but not uncommon in southwest France). Of those who were conscripted, one out of five failed to return, and a village of 2,267 inhabitants suffered the loss of 80. Amid this slaughter, about the time of the 1917 mutinies, a ray of sunlight shone through—the American soldiers arrived, with General Pershing announcing, "Lafayette, we are here!" The soldiers landed at Le Havre, at Cherbourg, at Nantes, and some arrived in different parts of the region around Pontlevoy, where they were trained and equipped. A large American camp was established at Gièvres between August and December 1917. At the dispatching center in Blois, three to ten thousand soldiers a day began arriving in January 1918 for dispersal throughout the southwest of the department. Besides the major depots at Salbris and Saint-Aignan, there were twenty-six military stations, as well as instruction centers and military hospitals, including those at Pontlevoy.

The training regiment was greeted with watchful interest by the inhabitants, especially children, who soon discovered Black-Jacks, a kind of chewing gum. The main barracks were set up on the Sambin road, near Thenay, and General Pershing went there to inspect his troops. The colonel took up quarters at Billeux, and Pontlevoy billeted a military band.

A military station occupied the site of the post office, a company of machine gunners was installed at La Garette, a nearby château, and soldiers lived at the school, chosen as the site of the military hospital. Some of the troops were billeted with local residents, and each house posted on its front the number of officers, noncoms, and soldiers staying in

it. As late as 1986, the west end of the rue de la Grefferie still bore the name Washington Avenue. Under the trees by the Grefferie hung sacks of sawdust for use in bayonet practice. In the little park, a trench was dug in the field so soldiers could practice throwing hand grenades. There was even a gas chamber where one could test the seal on one's mask and get used to wearing it; the photographer's son tried it out. During parade exercises, the village children followed the soldiers with brooms on their shoulders.

Two things about the Americans seem to have particularly impressed the locals: they had no beards and, as the old-timers put it, "they had gold-plated pusses." People in rural France found gold teeth a novelty as well as extravagant in appearance. Most of the village men had beards or mustaches, but the Gillette safety razor introduced by the Americans contributed to the disappearance, within a few years, of the "cabbage scrapers", as the village barbers were known, and to the removal of many beards and mustaches. The shopkeepers found the soldiers to be good customers; G. Chenneveau, for one, sold them the highest quality flashlights.

The Americans knocked off military drill at 1700 hours (five in the evening).

They then poured into the cafés and restaurants, where they loved to eat omelets. Many ate standing on the sidewalk or on the stairs. Lights-out was signaled by the call of a small trumpet.

What impressed the villagers of Pontlevoy above all about Americans was their modern mode of transportation. In 1917 the Americans already had tractors equipped with two hitches and front wheels that could turn at a right angle. The villagers also learned about the movies through the American troops. Lured by the announcement of show times, posted in the town hall, villagers gathered to watch the film in the school's riding ring. Jacques Clergeau went with his grandfather, though neither one could understand a thing, as "it was in American." One day the young Clergeau found a film on the Mexican war so gripping that he gnawed on his nice linen hat.

A Pontlevoy street photographed by Louis Clergeau before 1914.

The spires of the church of Saint-Pierre and the chapel at the Catholic boarding school.

PONT-LEVOY — Le Collège, façade de l'Abbaye

Cliché et édition Clergeau, Pont-Levoy

The south facade of the abbey, which is 262 feet (80 meters) long and was built in 1704.

PONT-LEVOY — Château des Bordes

Cliché Clergeau, Pont-Levoy

The house of a large landholder, some two miles northwest of Pontlevoy.

Formerly a farm-school in the nineteenth century, La Charmoise was photographed by Clergeau in 1905. The brick and stone manor has preserved its sixteenth-century stair tower; the building encloses a square interior court and is surrounded by a large moat with a stone bridge on the west side. Edouard Malingié, a former pharmacist from Lille, settled here in 1834 and developed a hybrid variety of sheep, which he named the Charmoise, after the house.

Tractor-driven threshers were beginning to be seen in 1926. Here, Gaveau, the owner of a threshing operation at Sambin, has set up on the Marié farm northeast of Pontlevoy. The long belt that powers the thresher can be seen extending from a pulley on the tractor.

The Serreau-Pinon family
during the 1907 harvest.
Harvester-binders had
started to come into use a
few years previously; this
one, drawn by two stout
Percherons, was probably an
American-made Wood
binder. The young woman
holding a rake and wearing
a long-sleeved blouse and
long skirt perhaps came out
to the field to bring food.
The earthenware jug carried
by another woman kept
water cool by evaporation.

Woodcutters at Phages,
a hamlet near Thenay,
make bundles of firewood
from the trimmings of
a stand of young trees.

pp. 28–29:
Threshing provided an
occasion for general
gaiety and a holiday
for the children.

The workshop of Joseph Léger in 1906. Like practically all blacksmiths, he turned his hand to repairing farm machinery—here, an American-made harvester-swather.

In this remarkable pyramidal composition of grape harvesters, depth is provided both by the cart at left and by the overlapping figures at right. No element in this photograph's structure—for example, the ladder, emphasized by the leg and left arm of the figure at left, nor the young man and the dog in the foreground—seems to be haphazard.

A crew of grape harvesters
at Saint-Romain-sur-Cher
in 1923. The three men
with baskets on their
backs were assigned
to carry the grapes
to a cart on which tanks
had been installed.

Firmin Meunier (center) and his portable wine press in 1902. The press was rented out to farmers who had none of their own. Louis Clergeau's father is at right, and next to him is Coco, the postmistress's dog. Behind the grape crusher and the barrel with its ashwood hoops is a magnificent barn, whose front section consists of wooden bars set between structural timbers and daubed with clay. One of a set of three buildings, it is today a garage.

Among this group of vine grafters in 1902 is Firmin Meunier (center, with cap), also the owner of a portable wine press, shown opposite. The grafters had a great deal of work at the time, as they had to rebuild the vineyards after they were ravaged in the phylloxera outbreak. One child is sitting on an old case of Aiguebelle chocolate, a popular brand at the time (along with Vinay, Menier, and Poulain).

The exit from the underground tufa quarries at La Rolandière (township of Bourré) on the village's east side. On the platform, along the main road, blocks wait to be loaded.

One of the patrician houses in Pontlevoy. Built in the first half of the nineteenth century, these generally belonged to rich families with a child attending the Catholic boarding school and served as peids-à-terre for seeing the boy during his vacation. They often had a modest garden in front and, like this house, a large park in the back.

Before 1914, the Chaumont
road was still unpaved.
The photograph shows
the direction in which
the competitors in the 1908
bicycle race would
be coming.

Emerging from the small woods southeast of Pontlevoy, the "steam tram car" heads toward the Montrichard road.

A dog cart at the station in 1922. Dog carts were mainly used by women and the elderly to trundle heavy loads such as laundry to and from the wash house or to take goods to market. Madame Grandvonnet was the last to use them for transporting freight.
For many years she brought the outgoing mail from the post office at Thenay to the Pontlevoy train and carried back the mail for that village.
The dogs, who liked to race ahead, more than once tipped over passenger and cargo.

The old train chugs into Pontlevoy's station, built when the tramway was first put into service in 1900.

pp. 38–39:
The crowd on hand at the station, at about 2:30 P.M. on Monday, August 14, 1910, to greet the prefect arriving to inaugurate the Pontlevoy airfield. A reception was scheduled at the town hall for 3:00, which the government representative would reach by making his way down the rue de Blois, festooned from end to end. After an exhibition at the airfield, "a banquet for subscribers at 3.50 francs a plate" rounded off the day.

A squadron of Blériot belonging to the military, photographed in 1912 in front of the new hangars.

This production model "Goupy bi-monoplane" had offset wings with two movable flaps at the wing tips and the Blériot's "pulled wheel" drive train. This is the plane that belonged to the pilot Divetain, photographed on May 25, 1911, during the Paris-Madrid air race. It would flip on takeoff.

In 1912, a Bleriot two-seater belonging to the military was photographed a few seconds before the order to "let go" was given. Note the three colors on the fin, the self-steering landing gear, and the five-liter gasoline can used to fill the tank. The soldiers are holding the airplane as it reaches full throttle, thus doubling the struts. On hearing the command, they will all let go at once, helping the airplane to a faster and safer lift-off.

Divetain's aircraft in the 1911 Paris-Madrid air race flipped on takeoff. This Goupy n15, built by the manufacturer in Issy-les-Moulineaux, had two offset wing surfaces and two movable ailerons at the end of either wing.

Airplane builders were constantly making modifications to their planes, often at the client's request, and clients would sometimes name the planes after themselves with the builder's consent.

A Voisin biplane after
a crash, in 1910.
The airfield still
had a ditch around it
at the time, which could
cause an airplane
to capsize if the takeoff
was too long. On the back
part of the wings, one can
see strange vertical ailerons
that rose as airspeed
increased.

pp. 44–45:
The facilities at the airfield
on August 15, 1910.
In 1912, two hangars
would be built for military
aircraft and a third added
later, all at right angles

to the road, in the grassy
area at right. From left
to right, we can make
out the Voisin biplane,
the Blériot, and the Goupy
belonging to the school
of aviation.

A Breguet biplane belonging
to the military in 1912.
This unusual model, with
its four-bladed propeller,
was developed in 1910.

Opposite:
A foreign student pilot
seated in a Blériot
in 1912. In front of him
is the gas tank made of
copper; above is a metal
support with guy wires
to stiffen the wings,
only the leading edges
of which are stiff, and
running cables for warping
the wing (a function
provided today by the
moving ailerons on either
side of the tail).

Some of the planes
already look perfectly
modern in form and
dispose of a respectable
amount of power.
This 100-horsepower
Charles Nieuport model
(the "100 HP"), which
belonged to the military
and was photographed
in September 1912,
would eventually be made
in a three-seater version.
A teacher from the school
is among the civilians
who came out to gawk.

The Americans began arriving in Pontlevoy in January 1918.
One of them was photographed here in a sidecar in front of the Café du Commerce in 1918.

The wedding of a soldier in uniform (1919).

A family photographed in 1920. During this period, Louis Clergeau made many portraits of this type, which were necessary in order to obtain the pensions of fathers or sons killed in the war.

A boy dressed up for first communion. It is 1922 and he wears the military decorations of his father, who died in World War I (the *croix de guerre* and *médaille militaire*).

The American military band in Pontlevoy, here seen in January 1919,
gave concerts almost every week on the place du Collège.
The room on the upper floor served as the soldiers' club, and the one below was
used for performing plays and showing movies.
At one celebration, J. Clergeau remembers having seen a black soldier play a violin made out of a stringed
broom handle. The brasses, which include the sousaphone, tuba, and French horn, were a particularly
important part of the band.

Twenty-seven years after their first stay in Pontlevoy, the American troops are welcomed back to the village on October 5 or 6, 1944. A delegation from the Blois health department is turning from the monument to the dead

The famous luncheon of the 1927 cavalcade at Pouillé. The procession went first to Sambin to collect funds, then to Thenay (where the collection yielded nothing), and finally to Pouillé.

In the foreground are several members of the municipal band and the La Pontilévienne club, G. Chenneveau among them, disguised as huntsmen. On the other side of the table are members of the Celebrations Committee. At the near corner, in a smock and hat, is M. Potreau, the bandleader, next to a milliner from Dolidon's, and Babouin, the well digger.

A Society on the Brink
of Great Upheavals

A Way of Life Tied to the Land

The Importance of the Schools

Religious Observances
and Secular Events

The Art of the Festival
and Conviviality

A Way of Life Tied to the Land

Those who held the upper hand in this society, as the photographs make clear, derived their power from the land. On the highest level were the big property owners, often members of the nobility, such as the Berthouins in Saint-Gilles, and all those who lived in a château or a manor house, for instance, La Mahaudière (to the north) or La Garette (to the south). Next came the wealthy farmers, the "masters" and "mistresses," as they were called, such as Achille Minier or Charles Tauvin, who was descended from three generations of local growers. Large farms such as Le Billeux, La Belle Etoile, La Pommeraie, Le Pin, and La Féalerie, which belonged to Charles Tauvin, were run with the help of substantial farm crews, which are only partially represented in the photographs. The Minier farm had a cowherd, a dairy-maid, and three or four carters including a head carter, although this did not keep Achille Minier from sometimes going on foot into the Berry region to buy cows. Farmer and farmhand seem to have lived on good terms, as did employer and employee in the village. Farm workers were often included in a farmer's family picture, and every photograph of a store

included the help, who often lived with their employer as part of the family. On the feast day of Saint Eloi, the patron saint of farmers and artisans, all employees were invited to a banquet organized by their employers. The night before, the workers would arrange for the gardener to create an emblem of the enterprise and hang it over the employer's door; they would then summon their boss by firing a gun, and he was bound to stand the happy group a drink.

On Trinity Sunday, when a large fair was held, one could rent oneself out. Carters wore the braided strand of a whip, and shepherds a tuft of wool. The bargain was agreed to orally and sealed when the farmer gave a coin to the hireling, who then had eight days to return it if he did not show up. Some thought to lay by a tidy sum by making the rounds of the various fairs but soon found themselves up before the justice of the peace in Montrichard.

The market, which was virtually the domain of the farmers' wives, presented a wealth of opportunities for socializing. In the summer it took place on the fairgrounds, while from All Saints' Day to Easter it was held partly in the school square (the poultry market) and partly in the square in front of the post office (everything else). Prices were unregulated,

and the costermongers often lowered them as the day wore on.

Early in the twentieth century, towns began increasing in population while the countryside emptied. In 1911, 56 percent of the French were living in rural areas, though the war made terrible inroads into that sector of the population. Industrial activity already employed a third of the French in 1913. The railroad, though late in reaching Pontlevoy, was an important factor in developing trade, bringing in products such as synthetic fertilizers, chemical applications for vines, sewing machines, bicycles, and motorcycles from the industrial regions. Many believed that progress would soon bring prosperity and justice to the nation as a whole, and the future was looked on with great hope. This future was heralded in numerous technical and artistic expositions and other kinds of celebrations. One such was the aviation celebration presided over by the departmental prefect on August 14 and 15, 1910.

The great strides made in chemistry brought about improved soils and increased yields. The Pontlevoy plain, which had traditionally been sheep-grazing country, like Beauce, now became farmland on which grain was grown. Great strides in mechanical engineering completed the modernization process. At the end of the nineteenth century, the reaper gave way to a harvester invented in 1870 by Johnston, an American, then to a harvester-swather that gathered the grain in a swath, though it still had to be tied by hand. By 1902 the first harvester-binders were coming into use, and Louis Clergeau photographed the one on the Alleu farm (which, unfortunately, was later damaged). Competition in this field was very fierce, but American equipment seems to have dominated. Brand names included Adriance, Wood, and McCormick, named after the inventor of the mechanical reaper. In 1902, threshing required a heavy traction engine and a threshing machine pulled by three horses. There were 51,000 threshers in France in 1892, and the number jumped to 480,000 by 1929.

Many blacksmiths, who traditionally repaired farm equipment, became dealers for the new machines. In Pontlevoy, the blacksmiths Rethoré and Léger prospered as the representatives of, respectively, McCormick and Deering. G. Chenneveau's father, however, represented a local French make, Planeau, which folded, and the blacksmith's son, like many others in his situation, turned to the repair and sales of bicycles and motorcycles. G. Chenneveau became the local representative for Dilecta bicycles, manufactured at Le Blanc.

The "horseless carriage," for its part, came into being at the very end of the nineteenth century, and the chauffeur, a word that originally applied to the stoker who had to heat (*chauffer*) the fire to start the steam engine, now generally wore a leather coat, a flat cap, and a pair of boots. The internal combustion engine reached a maximum speed of 40 miles per hour (64 kilometers per hour) in 1900, increasing to 63 mph (101 kph) in 1906. The famous Model T Ford went into production in America in 1909, and

by 1912 there were one hundred thousand of them on roads all over the world. Blacksmiths in the Pontlevoy area who had moved up to repairing bicycles and farm machinery by 1914 were starting to repair the new "automobiles" by 1920.

Airplanes and automobiles were being built in Pontlevoy in 1910, on the site of a former sugar beet factory. As in aviation, single prototypes of cars were made at that time. One such was the Luxior, which belonged to G. Chenneveau's father in 1912. The first to own a horseless carriage were Henri de Belot, who drove a De Dion; the blacksmith Rethoré, who kept his machine a long time to visit the airfield and watch the planes circling; and the farmer Minier, who lived in the village.

The Importance of the Schools

The Benedictine abbey, whose tradition as an educational institution goes back to its founding, ran a boys' secondary school from 1644 to 1776. In 1715 it became a royal school, and under Louis XVI a royal military academy. It was afterwards turned into a Catholic boarding school, known as the Collège de Pontlevoy, which became very well known. In 1904, when the separation of

church and state became law, it shut down, to reopen in 1905 with teachers who had been expelled from the seminaries of Blois and La Chapelle-Saint-Mesmin (Loiret). These were replaced in 1930 by Assumptionists, who in turn handed the school over to the Catholic diocese in 1934. The Germans burned down the school buildings in June 1940, and a center for vocational training operated there from 1942 to 1949, finally closing in 1950. The site was used from 1969 to 1971 as a vocational center for the rural trades, which was supplanted by a trade school for road transport that continued until 1995. The high point in the school's history was therefore the nineteenth and early twentieth centuries, when its alumni referred to themselves as "Pontlevoy graduates." In the nineteenth century the name Pontlevoy conjured up the image of a boarding school for the sons of the aristocracy, and in the twentieth of one that provided a strict but effective Catholic education.

When France was finally consolidated as a republic after 1873, the education of its citizens became an issue for reform. Laws passed in 1881 and 1882 made primary education free, compulsory, and lay. In villages all over France, new schools were built, and Pontlevoy saw a boys' school open its doors on the ave-

nue Malingié and a girls' school on the Contres road. By creating a teachers' corps (they were known as the "Black Hussars of the Republic") and by affirming the principle of equal education for all, the government sought to promote certain ideals, such as the belief in progress and in the general possibility of upward social mobility, and to lay the groundwork of a new morality. Citizenship was now to be acquired by apprenticing oneself to a qualified worker, the teacher, who offered not only an education but also instruction in gymnastics and preparatory military training. The republican myth of the citizen-soldier held sway in Pontlevoy until 1914. Boys who prepared for the military at school and practiced gymnastics at La Pontilévienne, the local athletics club, on receiving their certificates could choose a career in the military, and the best among them become officers. Between the two wars, one became a colonel, another a captain.

Girls were to be educated under the Republic as well and given the same social opportunities. The Girls' Primary School was the first to be built, followed in 1884 by the exalted establishment of the Ecole Supérieure de Filles on the Montrichard road. It seems to have been created in response to the Catholic boys' school, just as the private Saint-Gilles school on the Blois road formed a pendant to the lay state school.

Religious Observances and Secular Events

At the beginning of the century, the church and the secular state constantly jousted over the moral and social education of the French citizen. The church held processions and pageants, such as the one organized by the Catholic association of Thenay; the state mounted a panoply of Republican theatrics in the form of official functions, lay societies, and sporting events. The parish church bells that sounded the hour were seconded by the clock belonging to the boarding school, which had no clock face and was set a minute fast by the man who wound it so that it would ring before the clock at the new town hall, which was installed in 1911 at the top of a small steeple.

The religious and the profane necessarily mix in any procession, with the church banners advancing like military standards. Pontlevoy was host to regular processions, such as those held on Corpus Christi and to celebrate first communion, but events such as the anniversary of Abbé Roland's fifty years

in the priesthood in 1910 provided the occasion for additional pageants.

Two processions celebrated the festival of Corpus Christi. On the first Sunday, a procession organized by the parish church formed after mass, proceeding from the church to the boarding school chapel, where it made its first stop. The dean of religion led it from the chapel gate to the "lower door," the gate onto the Bourré road, making further stops at *reposoirs*, or street altars for the monstrance, on the fairgrounds and the place de la Poste before regaining the church and breaking up. A sign of the changing times, the procession was disrupted in 1914 for the first time by a gathering of opponents to the church demonstrating between the town hall and the post office.

The main event of the festival, the parade of the Eucharist through the streets in the late afternoon, organized by the boarding school, was held on the second Sunday. Clergeau's photographs show that the outer walls of the school were hung with white sheets that the young girls and nuns of the sewing circle had decorated with floral ornaments. The procession left by the gate opposite the church and was met by the curate on the steps, where it stopped at a first *reposoir*. Marcelle Clergeau described this procession with its unvarying order in a text called "Nostalgia": "The cross, the banner of the Virgin, and the members of the congregation came first. The town band came next, then the banner of the Angel Saints accompanied by its congregation and the student body, followed by the principal and all the teachers. Finally, leading the canopy carried by the older students and accompanied by the first communicants carrying lanterns came four priests in gold-embroidered vestments."

Ahead of this cortege, two rows of little flower boys wearing white crowns (one side dressed in blue, the other in red) threw flower petals down in front of the Holy Sacrament on a signal given by a clapper, while those carrying the thuribles turned to incense it.

After this group came those who worked at the school, the men first and the nuns who directed the domestic work after them, with the general population of Pontilevians bringing up the rear. The procession reentered the school grounds by the gate below the terrace, where the altar to Saint Joseph stood, and then went into the garden under the quincunx to the *reposoir* of the Holy Angels.

From 1911 down to the present day (with the exception of the years during World War II) an athletic club, La Pontilévienne, has played an active role in the history of the village. It consists of a number of groups that practice the sports of the time. France's defeat by Germany in the Franco-Prussian War of 1871 underlay the creation of this and similar clubs in nearby villages, which were formed to prepare the men of France to even the score. As the club's insignia still stated in 1925, it offered activities in "gymnastics, marksmanship and military training." The men who founded it were enrolled as reservists in officers' candidate school, at a time when the possibility of war loomed more and more threateningly. The first meeting was

held on March 16, 1911, and at a second general meeting on March 18, the tobacconist Fernand Testut, a former colonial, was appointed head. The teachers who gave preparatory military courses and evening classes for adults there after school played an important part in it. The club included representatives of all the trades and all the social classes: a doctor, a blacksmith (Marcel Léger), a notary's clerk (Papin), a farmer and former master sergeant (Boisbourdin, whose son and daughter-in-law would later figure prominently in the club's annals), another farmer (Marie Lebert), a cartwright (Briquet), and so on. This club formed a counterpart to the older "curate's athletic association," known as La Vaillante, which would not survive the war. Its members were outfitted as soldiers, their uniforms paid for through a subscription fund supported by a few wealthy families, which made it attractive to the sons of poor families; four of the eleven Lauron brothers belonged. La Pontilévienne had an advantage over La Vaillante in that it could count on the support of Joseph Paul Boncour, a graduate of the Pontlevoy boarding school, a former deputy, many times a government minister, and the senator for the department of Loir-et-Cher from 1931 to 1940, who on several occasions came to the society's aid.

The earliest uniform of La Pontilévienne documented in the photographs of Louis Clergeau features a white beret. Of the eighty from the township who died in World War I, 30 percent came from the society, and most died in 1914 executing bayonet attacks as part of the 113th infantry regiment.

In 1922, La Pontilévienne added a soccer division, called L'Etoile Sportive (Sports Star), in response to the enthusiasm shown for the sport introduced by the Americans. The Soccer Club of Pontlevoy was inaugurated in 1932, and although the club was to some extent a splinter faction, its members remained within the La Pontilévienne group. This state of affairs lasted only two years but produced its moments of sporting glory. Another sport introduced from America (through the teachers' training schools, the Ecoles Normales d'Instituteurs) led to a basketball division in 1935, under the assistant teacher Michaux. Other divisions would be formed after World War II, during which virtually all the members of the club either belonged to the Resistance or had run-ins with the Germans.

In 1921 La Pontilévienne pooled its funds to buy the firing range it had been renting since 1912 from the heirs of the Poulain family—a facility inaugurated, as it happens, at the same time as the town

The Art of the Festival and Conviviality

hall in 1912. Overall, this period witnessed a great enthusiasm for clubs and sporting activities. M. Boisbourdin, a former head of La Pontilévienne, remembers that during his student days only four out of a hundred boys did not belong to the club in some capacity.

The municipal band, another popular institution, played an important role in every public celebration and won its share of medals. At one point, some of the neighboring villages even had two, as in Sambin and in Monthou, which boasted both La Patriote and another band called La Vraie Patriote (the Real Patriot). At Saint-Romain, the White Band vied with the Red Band; in 1939, whenever red flags appeared at the town hall and parish church, the Whites would take them down the following night.

The centerpiece of Republican pageantry was the parade for Bastille Day, July 14, first held in 1877 and officially recognized in 1880, though it took some time to take hold. By the beginning of the century, the major elements of the ritual were in place: the singing of the *Marseillaise*, the procession of constituent groups, the flags with staffs aggressively topped with lance heads, and the fire brigade marching in place of the national guard. The entire population came out into the streets for the Fourteenth of July celebration, the festival of the Republic. "The Fourteenth of July embodied the intense patriotism of the lower and middle classes before 1914, whose zeal would feed the hecatombs of the First World War," as Bernard Dufour wrote in *La Pierre et le seigle* (Paris, 1977). The major republican figures in Pontlevoy gathered on that day. Festivities started the night before with a torchlight procession, artillery salvos (fired from a small cannon), fireworks, the launching of a hot-air balloon—at least, when the weather was not too warm and the risk of fire too high—and a gala ball.

On the following morning, four or five cannon shots signaled the imminent beginning of the parade, preceded by a distribution of aid to the poor. Merry-go-rounds provided entertainment during the pauses, and in the afternoon youngsters competed at climbing a greased pole. One of the more compelling games involved a tub of water hanging overhead and a person trying to perform a delicate maneuver with a long wooden pole while another pushed him in a cart; if the maneuver was performed incorrectly, the water came tumbling down on both their heads.

Even the most unfortunate in those days were buoyed by a certain *joie de vivre*, which is perhaps why the early years of the century are known as the Belle Epoque. Traditional institutions such the church were beginning to accept that this compartmented society, which had undergone no major changes in more than a century, harbored certain injustices. The religious and secular festivals provided a peaceful outlet for this rural society, at the same time that they cemented social relations. Serious aggression or jealousy were not yet in evidence. Simple things, processions and parades, public gatherings, and the company of friends around a well-provided table, provided pleasure. One might belong to the Société des Francs-Buveurs, or Free-Drinkers' Club, and unself-consciously have oneself photographed holding a bottle or a glass. On the other hand, no photographs were taken of elections. It never occurred to anyone to preserve the memory of an administrative action.

Both sporting events and school festivities were very much in vogue, and Clergeau has left an abundant photographic record of them. We find exhibitions of La Pontilévienne and its band on the fairgrounds, of the rhythmic gymnastics put on by the boys' school, and of the dances and ballets performed at their celebrations by the girls of the Ecole Supérieure. Bicycle races began to be held at the beginning of the century. G. Chenneveau, who was born in 1903, paid for his first bicycle with the contents of his piggy bank; it cost him 150 francs at a time when a coffee and brandy at the village cafés cost 35 centimes and a pint of beer 20 centimes. Between 1921 and the war, he organized both the Pontlevoy race and the Montrichard-Sambin hundred-kilometer event. The well-digger Babouin often won these races, and Clergeau immortalized him for posterity holding the victor's bouquet. When the townspeople of Sambin wanted to organize a bicycling event, Chenneveau, a bicycle repairman and dealer for Dilecta, tried to induce the company he represented to contribute a bicycle for the first prize. He was told that he did not sell enough bicycles to merit one, although, he remembers, the dealer in Blois had enough customers to receive a 10 percent discount as well as race prizes.

The conscription celebrations are an example of a tradition with recent origins. The term *conscript* referred to a man born in the same year as oneself, with whom one therefore expected to share a special camaraderie. The expression "He's my conscript" was used where today we might say, "He's my classmate." All the twenty-year-old men went together to the medical review board in Montrichard, where they stripped naked in front of the doctors to receive a detailed physical examination. Those who were found "fit for service" gathered proudly afterwards to celebrate the occasion, first fortifying themselves with badges, medals, and other trinkets bought at a store near the town hall. The celebration lasted a full week, during which the conscripts made sure to visit Clergeau's store and be photographed in front of the French flag. On years with many conscripts, they took up a collection and bought themselves a flag; one member of the group would keep it until the Fourteenth of July, when the flag would come out for the celebration and be passed on to another member. These celebrations provided occasions for considerable drinking. The group, banging on drums and blowing bugles, would make its way all around the countryside, eating at one farm after another. If a farm had no conscripts, the master was bound to set out the crock of potted pork and bread and wine. The custom underwent something of a revival when the "female conscripts," the young women born in the same year as the young men, were invited to participate in the festivities, at which they could not refuse to grant a few kisses.

The townspeople also gathered for meetings of the celebrations committee, which organized the cavalcades. Photographed extensively by Clergeau, these outings interwove themes from mythology, children's stories, politics (there was a float representing the Franco-Russian Alliance), and topical issues of the day (such as the *Presse-purée*, literally, a potato ricer, which alluded to the financial problems and fiscal pressures of the times). The inhabitants of Pontlevoy first began to hold their cavalcades in 1906, and they included sumptuous outdoor meals and banquets. One such festival honored Saint Eloi, an important holiday before 1914. Saint Eloi was the patron saint of agriculturalists, of artisans working in the agricultural sector, and of watchmaker-jewelers. On that day, a large crowd attended high mass; the saint received thanks for his many blessings, and then consecrated bread was passed out. Any leftover bread was brought to the town hall in covered baskets and eaten while one settled one's annual dues as a "member of the brotherhood of Saint Eloi." One of the perquisites of membership was a banquet to which women were not invited. The day ended, however, with a ball that had women dressed in gowns and a variety of dances, including the polka, the mazurka, quadrilles, and the skater's step.

People had great fun, perhaps desperate fun, given the storm clouds gathering over Europe at the time.

A group of grape pickers and
the vineyard's owner
(center). To his right,
a young man sits with
his elderly mother.

A thresher belonging
to Boileau, the owner
of a threshing service
in Pontlevoy, in 1921.
The mechanic is standing
on the self-propelled
steam engine at left,
oilcan in hand. At right
is the binder, his ties
hanging around his neck,
and in the center are
members of the harvest
crew with their rakes, sacks,
sheaves of grain,
and wheelbarrows for
carting coal.

A family of farmers (1906).
The man wears a *biaude,*
or smock, and the woman
a *caraco,* or loose jacket,
and the traditional bonnet
of Touraine.

This group photograph,
taken in 1907, is remarkable
in its precision: we see the
master's house slippers, the
dog's chain, the weave of
the textiles. The older
woman wears a smock dress
and the Pontlevoy bonnet.
As is often the case, the
window shutters have been
closed for the photograph,
probably at the photog-
rapher's request.

pp. 64–65:
The Billeux farm in 1906,
located in the village of
Pontlevoy, at one time had
been a sugar beet factory. A
haymaker and a harvester-
binder are visible in the
courtyard. The Tauvin family
owned this farm, which in
1910 became an airplane
and automobile factory
under Fernand Morlat.

The cooper Gougeard is pictured with his two apprentices in Pontlevoy in 1904. One is holding a cooper's adze, the tool that serves to cut a bevel on either end of the assembled barrel for inserting the head and the bottom.

Needing daylight for his photograph of the tailor Rabottin's workshop in 1903, Clergeau reassembled the workshop outdoors.

This 1906 photograph
of fruit pickers (the
Serreau-Pinon family)
offers a touching rural
scene. The peaches are
of the famous "High Wind"
variety, now no longer
available, which grew on
a vinelike tree. They were
so delicious, with such
flavorful juice, that they are
still recalled with
vivid emotion by those
more than fifty years old.

Threshing machines and their steam-powered drive engines, belonging to the Massay threshing
service of Vallières-les-Grandes, in 1908. Note the inappropriate poses of the young girl
holding the shovel and the two men pulling knobs on machines that are not running.

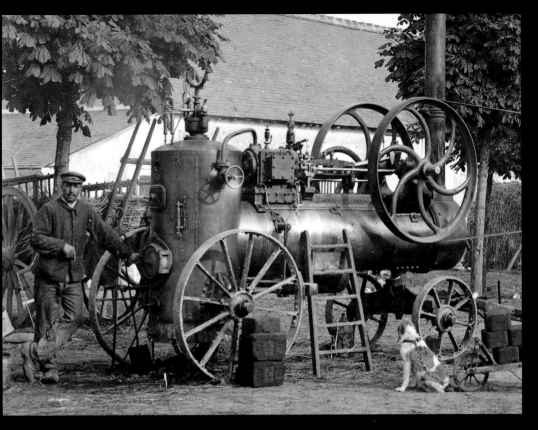

The boss of a threshing operation is shown near a portable steam engine in 1908.

In 1912, the village of Sambin could already boast a "motor-thresher," a thresher
with an internal combustion engine.

The Ford garage at the Belle-Etoile on the road to Blois was just a converted barn in
1923. At the time, cars of all makes were repaired there.

Part of the Chenneveau family in front of their bicycle and motorcycle store.
At right, a 1925 Motobécane.

Henri de Belot photographed on the grounds
of the Château de l'Alleu in 1910.

The blacksmith Louis Rethoré, left, had either the good fortune or the foresight to put his money
on McCormick farm machinery from the United States. He was selling McCormick harvester-binders even
before 1910. His son and grandson, right, continued to sell American equipment.

The wine maker and merchant Bled-Marteau from Saint-Romain, about 1923. His house is at left, the grape press at right, and in the center is the housing for those who worked in the vineyard and wheat fields.

The butcher Robert Princet (right, puffing out his chest), along with the counter help, the assistant butchers, and the salesman (who carries a bugle over his arm and a drover's stick), displays the fatted beef for the Mardi Gras celebration of 1923 at the butcher shop. Every butcher visited his suppliers at this time of year to choose the finest animal in their herds, then paraded it through the village decked in pompoms, ribbons, and flowers, taking up a collection as he went.

Alumni of the Catholic boarding school still remember the bleating of goat kids every Wednesday, when the market for poultry, eggs, and butter was held on the place du Collège. The market, visibly the domain of women, did not survive past World War II.

This photograph, taken from the window of the Clergeau house in about 1905, shows many women wearing bonnets, including the bonnet of Touraine, which has a large, flat knot falling over the nape of the neck and a ribbon to hold it in place.

The large wicker chests are intended for fowl, the baskets for carrying eggs wrapped in straw, and the baby carriages for animals, primarily rabbits and kid goats. To keep the animals from being startled, the hoods were raised and a large smock thrown over the opening.

The Café du Commerce on the place du Collège, 1930. A little higher and to the right was a bell that, at the beginning of the century, was rung to announce the start of the market. The butcher store clerk has crossed the square, a smile on his lips, to be immortalized by Marcelle Clergeau.

The Rochais bakery on the Grande-Rue in 1930. Both the corner bollard and the medieval carving of a monkey th[at] [g]ave the rue des Singes its name still exist at the corner of the rue du Colonel Filloux (formerly the Grande-Rue[)].

A novelty store, Sarradin, on the road to Blois in 1907. Items from Paris played an important role in spreading the spirit of modernism into the countryside. Bonnets were just giving way to hats. The old woman in this picture wears one of the last examples of a headdress once worn in Pontlevoy. This bonnet, possibly from the province of Berry, is tied under the chin, unlike the more commonly worn Touraine bonnet, which was attached to the chignon, or bun, with hairpins.

A hosiery and clothing store on the Grande-Rue. In 1930, the store also sold hats and ready-made clothing, including the worker's coat exhibited outside. The two children moved during the exposure, as did the grandmother on the right, trying to intervene.

The Fine company once again changed its name; by the time this photograph was taken in 1930, it had become the Dolidon store and added leather goods and silk to the notions and hosiery it originally offered. Thus was Parisian chic brought to the Pontlevoy region.

The boys from the Catholic boarding school, wearing linen hats, set off for a walk on a summer's day. In the rear, two teachers carry canes. The walks were long, and the band set the pace at an almost military clip.

The mother of the director
of the Ecole Supérieure,
the local state school
for girls, in 1909.

The teachers and students
of the tenth-grade class
at the Ecole Supérieure
in 1919. Mme Sévin,
the director, is seated
in the center.

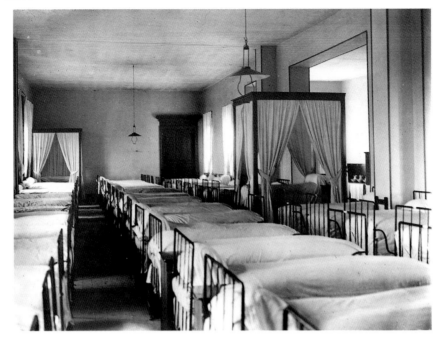

The dormitory of the Ecole Supérieure in 1921. The supervisors, who were women, had canopy beds with curtains that could be drawn for privacy.

A primary school cooking class at the Ecole Supérieure in 1921. Notice the cast-iron range, the lamp whose height could be adjusted with a counterweight, and the tidy organization of the spice jars.

A medical inspection at the Malingié school, the local state school for boys, in 1922. The instruments that had been in use indoors were brought out into the courtyard, and Clergeau somewhat humorously reconstructed the scene outdoors. This accounts for the photograph's aura of unreality, at the same time that it seems to present a slice of life.

Boys of the Malingié school perform gymnastics exercises on the fairground in 1922.
The monument to Edouard Malingié would subsequently stand on the left corner of the square.

During the festivities
organized in 1936
by L'Espérance,
the alumnae association
of the Ecole Primaire
Supérieure, the local
girls' school, students
act out a scene from
the play *L' Absent*.

The outdoor performance
of a play by the Ecole
Supérieure in 1921.
Today the school belongs
to the Department of
Health and Social Services.

A group of performers
pose with parasols during
the Espérance festivities
in 1936.

Prize-giving day at
the Saint-Gilles private
school for girls in 1911.
Marcelle Clergeau,
the photographer's
daughter, is the second
child to the right
of the teacher at left,
standing in the third
row, her long hair tied
with ribbons.

A group of priests,
with the Abbé Rolland
in the center, on the day
that celebrated his fifty
years in the priesthood.
Monsignor Mélisson,
the bishop of Blois,
is to his left. Also
present are a number
of canons, with their
white vestments,
red capes, and blue
sashes; the Abbé Vié,
the director of the Catholic
boarding school (a former
professor at the Saint-
Mesmin seminary,
he would become
the bishop of Monaco);
and several notable church
benefactors.

The Corpus Christi
procession organized
by the Catholic boarding
school in 1914. For this
procession, unlike that
of 1908, white sheets
with floral decorations
line the walls. The order
of the participants and
banners is unchanged.

pp. 90–91:
The 1910 procession
celebrating the Abbé
Rolland's fifty years in
the priesthood leaves
the church, heading
toward the school chapel.

The La Pontilévienne athletic club in 1920. The white berets that the members originally wore have been replaced by caps.

FANFARE PONTILEVIENNE
Concours de BARNEVILLE
1ᵉʳ PRIX de LECTURE A VUE
1ᵉʳ PRIX d' EXECUTION
1ᵉʳ PRIX d' HONNEUR
1ᵉʳ PRIX de SOLISTE

The Pontlevoy municipal band in 1927.

The full complement of La Pontilévienne, consisting of both gymnasts and military band, in 1912, a year after the athletic association was founded. The members perform exercises in front of the old town hall (today's post office), which at the time had been closed for several months and was serving mainly to display advertising.

The Pontlevoy fire brigade in 1929. The captain was a local farmer.

The Fourteenth of July parade down the Grande-Rue as it reached the photographer's store. Leading the town band and the firemen are a group of boys in shorts and straw hats. On the right is a water pump set in the wall of the Catholic boarding school. The wheel is still there, but the handle has been removed in deference to the safety of passersby.

The bandwagon, escorted by horsemen in dragoon outfits, during the 1906 cavalcade.

The float of the chimney sweeps during the cavalcade of Sambin in 1921.

The *La Réclame* float in the 1907 cavalcade.

pp. 98–99:
A famous float in the 1938 cavalcade called the "Presse-purée" (potato ricer) alluded to the financial problems and fiscal pressures of the times.

A goat cart in the 1938 cavalcade.

**The Aeolian float proceeds down the Grande-Rue
during the cavalcade of 1938.**

The queens of the 1938 cavalcade on their float. Notice the "HX" on the license plate, the old designation for the Loir-et-Cher department. The Latil truck on the Grande Rue arrives in front of the Clergeau store on the place du Collège.

A float in the May 1938 cavalcade. The decorated vehicle is a Renault.

In the 1932–33 season, the Pontlevoy Soccer Club became the second-division champions for Central France. The club's directors, Babouin (the town well digger and a bicycle racer) and Chenneveau (the garage owner and a drum player in the La Pontilévienne band as well as a bicycle race organizer) are on the right, holding the banner. The Lauron brothers were members of the team.

A group of friends
photographed on a special
occasion in 1921.
Three of the young
men wear the uniform
of La Pontilévienne,
the sports and military
prep association.

In a bicycle race of 1908, the cyclists approach the café near two blacksmith shops on the Chaumont road (today's rue Auguste Poulain).

Babouin, a well digger whose wife ran a café across from the blacksmith on the Chaumont road, poses after winning a bicycle race in 1924. Part of his sports outfit was made from a pair of breeches.

The start of a bicycle
race in front of
G. Chenneveau's on
the Chaumont road
in 1932. The sign for
his bicycle store can be
seen in the background
at right, while he himself
is in shirtsleeves at left.
At right is the former
bicyclist Babouin on
his motorcycle. As
the road had to be
closed off for the race,
Chenneveau only allowed
Clergeau fifteen minutes
for the photograph.

The 1902 conscripts with their flag. The central banner of the flag, where the year was written, changed every year.
It began as a Zouave; in 1902, it changed into two cannons; in 1904, a two-headed eagle; and from 1906 on, a bust of the Republic carrying flags and palm leaves.

The 1912 conscripts. Using
their musical instruments,
they would make noise
in the countryside
to get themselves invited
to lunch by farmers.

The conscripts of 1911 with their knickknacks, ribbons, flags, and musical instruments. Making the rounds of the local farms for a drink and a meal, the conscripts would announce their presence with their noisemakers.

The "Francs-Buveurs," a drinking club, photographed in front of the Café Bruneau in 1907.

Young men at a wedding
party in 1913. Top hats
were worn on formal
occasions; the fedora,
which we see here in the
company of a boater and a
cloth cap, was just starting
to appear. When we reflect
on the possible fate of
some of these young men
only a year later, the scene
takes on a deep poignancy.

Among the characters
assembled for the Minier
wedding at Fougères-sur-
Bièvre are, at right,
a cook and, at left,
a servant woman wearing
a strange fluted headdress.

A fiddler's services were
retained for this 1902
wedding.

French Families

Important Family Occasions

Inequalities

Important Family Occasions

After 1918, the photographer generally was called in only a few times during a lifetime to memorialize important family events. He immortalized the heir a few weeks after his birth, lying naked on a pillow. The baptismal ceremony itself was never photographed, due either to insufficient light or to discretion, but group photographs were taken afterwards in which the mother holds the baby in her arms and the godmother the bouquet presented her by the godfather. This holds equally for the first communion ceremony, which was rarely photographed at the beginning of the century; instead, we see group photographs of the participants or their procession as they passed in front of the school. Things began to change in 1925.

Weddings remained the most important family celebration. For most they offered a brief respite from the daily round of hard work and sacrifice. The wedding ceremony provided the opportunity to reaffirm friendships and tighten the bonds of family and social obligation; it also functioned as an arrangement between two clans, since the couple often came together outside the private domain.

Death itself would not necessarily remove one from the reach of the photographer, as he was often called in to take the last photograph of a child in his best clothes or of a priest on his deathbed. On the other hand, Clergeau seems never to have photographed a funeral procession—perhaps because burial was often conducted as a civil ceremony in this part of Loir-et-Cher, where a certain opposition to religion had developed and churchgoers were relatively fewer than in the neighboring regions.

Inequalities

Photographs attest to the inequality of families. The inequalities of wealth and status present within a group or between one group and another can often be detected by looking at the clothes and jewelry. The standard photographs taken of wedding parties and other functions also allow us to trace the birth and progress of new fashions. At the start of the century, the peasant costume was everywhere the same: a *biaude* (smock) for the men, and for the women a *caraco* (loose jacket), a long black skirt protected by a *devantiau* (apron), and a bonnet. Then bonnets gradually disappeared and millinery fashions became more complex. Hats with feathers and flowers proliferated and their size increased. Skirts became heavy and voluminous, often with pleats, and women carried showy parasols. This phase proved only momentary, to be swept away in the years after World War I. Starting in 1925 and certainly by 1928, feminine styles grew lighter and skirts shorter, which made them more "chic." On their engagement, men began to wear signet rings, as was the custom in the cities. Women, who had originally worn their wealth on their person (earrings, charms, a fob with a watch tucked into a small pocket), now abandoned heavy ornaments in favor of smaller but more varied jewelry. The young tried to break away from local styles and array themselves in "Parisian chic," as they found it at Fine's (now renamed Sarradin) or in the catalogues of Parisian department stores, which were readily available through local outlets.

Appearances to the contrary, rest and leisure activities remained rife with social and sexual inequalities. Recreation in the years between the wars was primarily pursued within the context of an association. One engaged in sports with the members of La Vaillante or La Pontilévienne, played music with a pipe band or a municipal orchestra, and took part in festivities through the Celebrations Committee, which organized balls, cavalcades, and banquets. Women were excluded from a number of these activities; their domain included the sewing circle and various good works. Certain societies were founded on a political or religious basis. In Thenay (and afterwards in Pontlevoy), the Catholic Association marched in the 1928 parade, and a socialist association, calling itself the Proletarian Social Economy, had itself photographed in 1909. Groups sometimes formed around simple pleasures, such as the Société des Francs-Buveurs of Pontlevoy (Free-Drinkers Club of Pontlevoy), who had themselves photographed in 1907, glass in hand, their banner surrounded by paper lanterns.

Others preferred more natural recreations, such as hunting or fishing. Anguilleuses Brook could only be fished in the mill ponds above Pontlevoy, but there was also fishing in "pits," such as at Cloudron. Those who owned cottages there invited their friends to visit. Only the very rich are likely to have traveled, except the owners of large farms, who seldom left their farms for a rest.

English embroidery was
very much in fashion in
1906. Little children from
the area's châteaux,
who wore white dresses such
as this, had their clothes
changed twice
a day—which accounts
for the many laundresses
employed in great houses.

Little girls hold their dolls,
shod in tiny boots (1902).

Toddlers and their toys,
photographed in front
of a rabbit hutch in 1907.
The baby at right has
a rattle, probably made
of silver and ivory, around
his neck.

The Bachelier family, photographed in 1906.

A baptismal party in 1909.

A grandmother and children in 1906. The children wear boots that had to be fastened with a button-hook. The little girl at right wears a magnificent embroidered collar made in England.

The grandmother wears a *caraco*, or loose jacket, and a *devantiau*, or pleated apron, around her waist to protect her skirt.

A grandfather and child in 1906.

At this wedding in 1930, everyone is smiling, and some of the children managed to remain spontaneous in front of the camera (one little girl looks at her nice clothes, another at the wedding pair). At left, a woman leans into the frame, as if in fear of being left out of the photograph.

A wedding party at La Charmoise in 1909.

pp. 122–23:
The Trotignon wedding in Saint-Romain, 1902. A handsome composition, with a soldier and a cavalryman on either side, and something of a wink in the inclusion of the figure seated in the hayloft. At left, two beautiful embroidered vests can be seen. Women mainly wore bonnets, but some were starting to "wear hat," an expression used by older women in the countryside to disparage those who were abandoning traditional headgear. Among the men we see only a single top hat but already two fedoras.

The wedding of a dragoon in 1911. Three women, in the second and third rows, wear the traditional bonnet of Pontlevoy.

A double wedding with both brides in short dresses (1928). How studied the composition, and what symmetry between the two wedding parties!

A bride and groom in 1928, the year brides started to appear in short dresses.

A family in the courtyard
of their house in 1920. This
interesting composition is
in two parts: a family core
that encompasses three
generations and includes
two small dogs, then, off to
one side, an old couple that
almost certainly does not
belong to the family
(the man wears a *biaude*, or
smock, and the woman a
caraco) and a young clerk.

Here is a family in comfortable circumstances, where the men sport bow ties and pocket handkerchiefs. They pose in front of their tufa house with well-kept garden in 1922. A half curtain hangs in the top part of the right window with embroidered curtains below, there are potted plants spaced at regular intervals, and a caged bird provides listening pleasure.

The eleven boys (of sixteen children) in the Lauron family in 1932.

The Lauron family with all sixteen children, photographed in 1919.

Firmin Meunier's family
in 1905. The elderly farmer
wears a *biaude*, or smock,
and the boys for the most
part floppy ties and dress
boots. Except for one
couple, all wear dark
clothes.

pp. 130–31:
A cooperativist group
founded on socialist ideals
in Thenay, 1909.

A remarriage in 1910.
The party is an intimate
one and all wear dark
clothes, except for
the young girl.

A family in 1906.
The woman on the right
wears a watch fob,
as many women did.

These artisans, who make
rush seats for chairs,
have written the date and
place of the photograph
in chalk on the wall
behind them. Pontlevoy's
name would be written
without a hyphen starting
at the end of World War II.

A hunting party in the Saint-Lomer woods, Thenay, 1923. The object of the hunt, which employed both dogs and beaters, is the badger in the foreground. Among the participants are the gamekeeper (wearing a raincoat), a policeman, and the mayor of Thenay (to the right of the policeman).

"Pit fishing" on the
Pontlevoy plain.

A fishing party at Cloudron,
east of the village, in 1911.
This idyllic scene features
fishermen in shirtsleeves,
a young dandy in a cap,
and men wearing jackets.
The women have come,
too, one having brought
her parasol, the other
her needlework. The
surrounding countryside
is planted with grape-
vine, and the fishing is
done in "pits," probably the
remains of old quarries.

A patrician family in
the park in front
of its house.

Fishermen taking their
ease in front of a tiny
house between
the vineyard and
the fishing pit. A shelter
and a hearth right by
the fishing hole,
no more than a mile from
the village, represents
the height of rural luxury.
This photograph is all
the more precious in
that it shows us the
equivalent of a vineyard
shed, freshly built from
Bourré stone.

The conscripts of the class
of 1955 have some fun.

Several Years Later...

Many years have passed since the time that Louis Clergeau, a young man filled with enthusiasm and talent, settled down in Pontlevoy and set out on his career as a photographer. It is Marcelle who would wind up this long history. The photographs she took during the 1950s, which would be her last, reveal that the village not only lived in the moment but also remained attached to its past, despite the profound changes that society experienced over the years.

The village and its surrounding countryside have preserved their authentic nature; an excessive urbanism has not come to spoil it. While communal social events have undoubtedly experienced a decline, they continue to be very important. Thus, for example, La Pontilévienne did not end after World War II. Starting in 1945, it opened membership to girls and created new divisions. Marcelle photographed the society in its entirety with its band on August 15, 1948, just before it left for a nearby town where it had been invited to participate in a celebration.

In July 1955, "Pontlevoy's big week" was organized. This fair, commercial in nature, filled the fairgrounds and its neighboring streets with numerous exhibition booths. Marcelle, shooting one of her last events, recorded each of the booths (recalling the images showing the facades of Pontlevoy's shops during the 1930s). The exposition focused on the agricultural and viticultural activities of Pontlevoy and the region, thus providing a window on the evolution of machines and techniques.

In the same year, the "conscripts" of 1955 posed for the traditional group picture, just as they had in the past. In another, more whimsical image, they are shown leaning against a splendid automobile decorated with graffiti.

With her extensive background in photographing weddings, Marcelle continued this activity to the end of her career, for which she utilized, as always, glass plates that were 18 by 24 centimeters. An image from 1961 demonstrates how much fashion had changed; in addition, the participants seem to smile more than before. With her usual concern for perfection, Marcelle made them keep their pose for a long time, something they still remember today with amusement.

In 1963, Marcelle retired. Her photographs reveal that Pontlevoy remained a convivial and authentic village whose history has been left to posterity.

The Benoist-Berlu wedding, in 1961. The family still lives in the area.

The full membership of the Société La Pontilévienne was photographed together in 1948.

Agricultural machines on display during "Pontlevoy's big week" in 1955.

The coopers' booth during "Pontlevoy's big week" in 1955.

The viticulturalists'
exhibition booth during
"Pontlevoy's big week" in
1955.

ACKNOWLEDGMENTS

Raymond Landin made the prints from the original negatives.
Nina Favard and Jean-Mary Couderc particularly wish to thank Jacques Clergeau
for his generosity, for his untiring helpfulness, and for bestowing on them the benefits
of his infallible memory of the past. They are equally grateful to Georges Chenneveau,
Jacques Pécard, Gilbert Boisbourdin, and Rolande Rivault for the invaluable information
and documents they so kindly provided. Profuse thanks as well to all the Pontilévians
who communicated their memories of the past, and, finally, to the Société des Amis
du Musée de Pontlevoy (represented by Nina Favard), as well as Paul Gottlieb,
without whom this book would never have come about.